NORTH WALES PRIVIES

Tai Bach Gogledd Cymru

Cariad ac Llgwn
1999

8. Se

NORTH WALES PRIVIES

Tai Bach Gogledd Cymru

by

J. AELWYN ROBERTS

COUNTRYSIDE BOOKS

NEWBURY • BERKSHIRE

ISBN 1 85306 535 8

Produced through MRM Associates Ltd., Reading
Printed by Woolnough Bookbinding Ltd., Irthingborough

CONTENTS

The Honourable Association of Privy Owners

A wise man tests the waters before joining group conversations. Talk politics, and many will sidle away. Talk religion, and unless it is at a church convention, the whole group will assume a Madame Tussaud-like posture. But if you talk of old fashioned, top or bottom of the garden privies, you could easily achieve stardom.

People seem to warm to you when you talk about this subject. Even at parties I have found men, glass in hand, edging from their own group to join another if the talk was about privies.

'I couldn't help overhearing what you were saying,' they confide. 'It reminds me of my old aunt. She used to tell us how they had a privy in the garden and the fun they used to have ...'

The author with a pair of round privies at Marford Hill.

Pensioned off. Soil, bucket and spade remain just in case, at Mynydd Llandegai, Bethesda.

I have to explain at this point that although this book is called *North Wales Privies*, 'privy' is an alien word to a Welsh person. This private place apart is called by many and various names in the English language, but in Wales it is different. If 100 Welsh people were asked to give the Welsh name for the WC, without a doubt as many as 99 would say 'Ty Bach'. The 'Ty' is pronounced as the *tu* in French and 'Bach' as in Johann Sebastian Bach, bless him. The name Ty Bach is written in the Laws of Prince Hywel the Good, who died in AD 950.

Welsh was my first language, my mother's tongue. When I write the word 'privy' in this book I will probably be thinking 'Ty Bach', and no doubt as I go along I will also be saying 'Ty Bach'.

When I began writing this book I was amazed at the number of people who wrote to me or phoned to say they knew of a friend who had a garden loo. They also regaled me with stories, told by grannies, of the adventure of going to the bottom of the garden, hand in hand with big sister, on a cold winter's night, with Father going first to light the privy candle or lantern and then taking up guard duty at a distance.

But the number of original unadulterated outside toilets has become surprisingly few. A spokesman for the National Trust told me: 'It was whilst searching for information for your book that I realised how very few of the many old houses we administer have retained their garden toilets.'

That is the bad news. The good news is that the owners of garden privies I have come to know are so very proud of their possessions and intend to look after them. They speak of them with warmth and loving care. You have such a welcome when you ask if perhaps you can have a little peep at their garden toilet. When you bring out a camera to take a photograph you are made to feel you have been accepted into their inner circle of friends!

Even the friends and neighbours of garden privy owners seem to enjoy a sort of vicarious fame and pride of ownership. Often it was the friends and neighbours who answered my media appeals for help. 'My friend has an old fashioned toilet in her garden,' they wrote, 'and *hers* is a listed building!' More often than not when I got there I found the building was not listed – although recently quite a number have been.

I rejoice in this new-found pride. It heralds the end of that mass destruction of redundant and pensioned privies. Heritage loos have been pulled down stone by stone, and two- and even three-holed seats have been thrown onto bonfires. Others have been modernised with pan and chain, or have just suffered a crude conversion into a shed for rusty tools.

An estate agent suggested to me that in the new millennium we might even see this new-found pride bringing about the end of the mode of dating properties with the names of the monarchical periods in which they were built. No longer will we read, 'The house is Elizabethan' or 'Victorian' or 'Edwardian'. Future estate agent terminology may just add the one, by then greatly sought after, phrase: 'This house has, in its spacious orchard, its own antique privy (circa 1850) in mint condition.'

As I visited privy after privy and met privy owner after privy owner, I wondered these owners had not ere now banded together in a sort of society or association of their own. I remember in the years after the war some of the Electricity Companies sponsored clubs that met monthly. These groups were called the 'Electrical Women's Associations' and all that the members had in common was their possession of an electric cooker or an electric washing machine. The people I have visited recently have a far greater common bond. There could be here an association waiting to be inaugurated: 'The Garden Antique Privy Owners Society'.

As a retired clergyman I know only too well the difficulty the Honorary Secretaries of clubs and associations have trying to find speakers for meetings., The GAPOS Hon. Sec. would not have to do this. Members could keep it going without inviting guest speakers by just swapping their own quaint lavatory tales. There is one I heard the other day and it is one that I am dying to tell.

Richard Ellis-Davies is a very old friend of mine. He celebrated his ninetieth birthday some time ago. Richard was a family solicitor and for many years was Deputy High Sheriff of Caernarfonshire. But this story concerns his childhood. His father was Member of Parliament for Caernarfon during the period of the First World War. He would come home from Westminster, by train, every Friday night and return on Monday morning. Always when he came home he would bring with him, from his London office, an accumulation of scrap paper for the children to draw on or to be cut up and used in the privy.

One Friday evening the MP dad brought home with him two high ranking fellow Members of Parliament, together with the usual pack of waste paper. His wife, taken aback by the advent of the two unannounced guests, handed the bundle of papers to Rosie the maid, saying, 'We can manage without that lot for a start. Take all this paper down to the Ty Bach, Rosie. Don't bother to cut it into squares; we can do that next week. Just take it out of the way for now.'

Rosie toddled off with paper and was back in no time. An hour or so later one of the London VIPs wended his way to the garden and towards the Little House at the bottom. He sauntered slowly as was the custom, bent down to smell each little rose, and ran his hand through the tufts of lavender and Old Man growing in profusion along the path. In two minutes he was back, doubled up with laughter. When the others in the drawing room saw him, they went to ask the cause of the merriment. But the big man could only point towards the loo and continue his howls of laughter.

So the whole party toddled along into the spacious privy and there it was on the wall as they entered. Rosie, taking the papers, had noted that some of them were war recruiting posters and she had thought it would be such a shame to use them all as wipes. So she had carefully pasted one of them on to the wall. It was a picture of a rather ancient General Roberts displaying the Victoria Cross he had won in the Boer War. Under the picture were the words:

HE DID HIS DUTY. WILL YOU DO YOURS?

Just right for the privy wall! (*Imperial War Museum*)

[1]

THE HISTORICAL BACKGROUND

Someone has said, and if I know anything about universities has received a PhD for saying it, that human beings excrete 10% of all they eat. How, I wonder, does anyone find out something like this? Does he actually ...? But enough!

What we do know is that this body waste, if not quickly disposed of, becomes a problem – a problem that has exercised the mind of mankind from the beginning of time,

It has been suggested that the Romans, who were capable of building such a luxurious system of baths and toilets in their cities and villas, must have been shocked at the way we Celts crouched down and did our business whenever, and wherever, we felt like it.

The type of lavatory that was built where soldiers were garrisoned as at Deva (Chester) and at Segontium (Caernarfon) was carefully designed. Communal seats surrounded a stone floor into which was set a narrow, gravity fed waste channel. Water entered from the top and flowed around the room, then dropped down into the main water channel that flowed below the seats. A small bowl set in the middle contained sticks with small sponges attached. These served to clean the Roman posteriors and could then themselves be washed clean in the water channel directly in front of the sitter. These mechanics were remarkably effective and formed the basis for public toilets throughout the Roman world.

The Romans were nothing if not matter of fact about the whole procedure. Even in Rome itself, chamber pots and commodes and buckets were just as much in evidence as in any town in Britain. These buckets and vessels were placed

Garrison latrines at a Roman fort, as they may have looked. Note the cleansing sponges sticking out of the bowl, used and rinsed each time. The water channel ran in front of, and then out of sight beneath, the sitting legionaries!

strategically along the streets of Rome so that the citizens, plebeians and patriarchs, could use them free of charge. As a matter of fact, the Emperor Vespasian (AD 69 – 79), the son of a moneylender, became perhaps the first person in Europe to realise there was brass in muck. He decided to sell, to the highest bidder, the rights to carry away and use the contents of the street vessels. These merchants would then resell the urine to cloth manufacturers to use as a cheap form of ammonia. The rag trade of the time (and for many centuries afterwards) used gallons and gallons of it to soften and bleach cloth so that it could absorb colour.

After the Roman Empire fell, centuries passed before any further attention was given to sanitation, although the same care that had been taken in garrison complexes was evident in the larger monasteries in North Wales – Valle Crucis near Llangollen and Maenan Abbey near Llanrwst. And the Celts had picked up a few wrinkles from their Roman conquerors. In the 10th century the Laws of Hywel the Good enacted that the court should appoint a kind of Minister of Urine, because urine was far too valuable a commodity to be thrown away. Every community also appointed its own 'Bismaer' or 'Dung Mayor' to arrange for the buying and selling of human excrement. The term 'Mayor' was perhaps a little derisory, but the holder was still regarded as a person of importance.

Later the Normans came and taught us how to build great castles and cathedrals and beautiful arches, but even these great builders and architects hadn't a clue about loo building. They scoured the whole of Europe for craftsmen to build their castles in Conwy and Beaumaris. But when it came to the question of sanitation, the best idea any of them could come up with was to build rows of niches into the walls, dig a hole through the outer wall of each niche, place a slate

The Conwy Castle garderobes – a line of twelve depositing waste outside the castle walls.

or wooden seat with a posterior-sized hole in it over that hole, and allow the excreta of hundreds of soldiers and townsmen to sludge its way slowly down the side of the castle walls to the moat below. These insanitary inventions were known by the distinguished name of 'garderobes'.

So it was not just the poor and humble that had to suffer the smells and the fevers and the suffering that went hand-in-hand with poor sanitation. Kings and queens and their courtiers shared the same fate. Poor Mary Queen of Scots, when she was imprisoned in Tutbury Castle in Staffordshire, sent this pitiful letter to a friend:

'As no house with so many low bred people in it as this, can be long kept clean, however orderly they may be, so this house, and I blush to have to say it, wanting proper conveniences for the necessities of nature, has a sickening

16

stench ever lingering in it. Every Saturday too, the cesspools must be cleared out, even to the one below my windows, whence come none of the perfumes of Arabia.'

There was of course no such thing as toilet paper, nor would there be for a long while yet. In the 15th century, John Russell's *Book of Nurture* laid down some guidelines for running a great house:

'See the privihouse for easement be fayre soote [sweet] and cleane. And that the bordes this upon be covered with fair cloth and greene. And the whole itself look no board be seen. There on a fair cushion the ordure no man to teme. Look there be blankit, cotyn, or lynyn to wipe the nether end.'

I'm quite sure the King's humble subjects in North Wales would not have been able to afford the luxury of 'blankit, cotyn, or lynyn' to wipe their nether ends. They would have had to be content with grass or leaves.

But North Wales had its mountains and rivers, its little streams and lakes. It became obvious from early times that the simplest way of disposing of human waste was by using these many little streams and rivulets. It could be said: 'Blessed is he that hath a stream running through his garden for he shall be thrice blessed.'

Possibly most of Wales' rural Ty Bachs were ones built directly over streams. The 'little house' would be built over the stream or running parallel with it. It would be constructed of wood, or stone, or brick. Inside, it would have a box seat with holes. The waste that passed through the holes would be washed away by the stream. There would be no smells, no unpleasantness and no maintenance. Families could ease themselves as hygienically as they do today – perhaps more so because the whole process was in the open air and there was never any mention of blocked drains or

The privy at Penmachno Woollen Mill that doubled as a bidet!

roddings. Blankit, cotyn or lynyn to wipe the nether end apart, many an old North Walian pleb, sitting on his two- or three-holer over a fast moving stream would have felt more royal than the king himself. Like the old miller at Penmachno Woollen Mill sitting on his throne above the river Machno. When the river was in flood this particular privy doubled up as a bidet!

Sometimes, though, even this happy solution could not resolve the disposal problem. For centuries contaminated water caused outbreaks of typhoid fever, cholera and other water-borne diseases that killed many, especially young children. Even in the late 19th century the city of Bangor was nearly rejected as a suitable place to build a University College of North Wales because there were so many outbreaks of water fevers in the area. The city and its new university-to-be, were saved only when a local sanitary

Bangor University, almost a casualty of water-borne diseases.

inspector discovered that at flood times the sewage of one small farm, situated above the new Bangor Reservoir, was filtering its way into Bangor's drinking water.

Urban dwellers not fortunate enough to have a stream or a bit of garden often remained dependent on chamber pots or slop pails. Each household must have had a good number of these utensils. When they were full and smelly, the owners would, very much like modern-day golfers, give one warning of intent. They would open the bedroom window or the front door and shout, 'Gardy loo!' ('Gardez-l'eau' – 'Watch out for water!') and then they would chuck the potty contents over the pavement (or pedestrian) below for the wind and the rain to dispel. The poet Dryden in 1650 wrote of the dangers of walking through town:

> 'Tis want of sense to sup abroad too late
> Unless thou first hast settled thy estate
> As many fates attend thy steps to meet
> As there are waking windows in the streets.
> Bless the good gods and think thy chance is rare
> To have a piss pot only for thy share.'

The very rich might have 'garderobes' in their manor houses or town houses, but it would be many centuries before the ordinary town or country dweller could consider an indoor loo – or would even want to, as we shall see in the next chapter. Meanwhile, the countryman could consider himself fortunate to possess even the tiniest of gardens. For many years when the call came they would just go out into the garden, find a fairly clean patch, dig a little hole, crouch down and fill it.

The earth closet obviated the need for a man to regularly prod and prog in his little garden to find a clean spot to dig a

20

new hole. The requirement was to select one spot only, a fair distance from the house. Here a huge deep hole could be dug, the soil removed and stacked close to it. A seat mounted on blocks would then be placed over the hole, and a weather shelter placed over the whole caboosh. When a member of the family evacuated himself in the new-fangled loo he or she would be required to shovel into the hole, before they left, some of the soil stacked outside.

Urban or semi-urban houses with small tiled backyards and not sufficient room to dig large holes – and indeed many country homes where digging a large hole was not welcome – would opt for a bucket closet. The same kind of raised seat, but in this case raised high enough for a large bucket to be placed underneath the hole.

But it was the indignity of it all that passes understanding – especially for the women. This was brought home to me once when I was vicar of Llandegai. We had managed to find a good camp site for some gypsies who were being thrown from pillar to post, and once the caravans had been arranged in tidy rows, the council workmen came to build a little row of privies at the bottom of the field. I received an SOS from the gypsy elders. Something had gone radically wrong. When I arrived at the camp they all escorted me to see the new privies and I was asked by the leader of the protest movement: 'Would you like your wife having to use a privy like these?'

I couldn't see at first what all the fuss was about. The little privies looked very tidy. And then it was pointed out to me – the doors. The doors had been cut about ten inches short of the ground, presumably to allow for ventilation. But the men pointed out to me it was not decent for other men to see the feet of their womenfolk as they sat on the privy seat. This was a complaint from people whose wives had, up to that day,

Reverend Henry Moule's patented design for a more hygienic earth closet.

been going off to the field a little beyond the camp and crouching down in the privacy of the trees. I had to concede that in some peculiar way they did have a point, and in any case the workmen could have used their commonsense and placed the doors to open on the blind side of the camp, not where all the users could be seen entering and leaving.

But our grandparents had to do more than just sit and expose their feet. In the country, when coming out of the earth closet they would have been required to use the often wet and soiled spade to shovel some of the soil from outside on to the 'what they had done' in the hole. Another recipient of a PhD has somehow been able to work out that, just by normal usage, two and a half tons of soil would be shovelled back into a normal lavatory hole in one year. This very often

22

John Parker's fully automatic earth closet, patented in 1870.

was a task that had to be carried out by shy young maidens attired in voluminous satin dresses. And if they used a bucket closet, there was always the time when the bucket was nearly full and mounting perilously close to the rim of the seat!

As so often happens, it was the inventive brain of a clergyman, the Reverend Henry Moule, in 1860, that brought relief to the crinolined ladies. He invented Earth Closet Mark II. Behind the seat the Reverend gentleman devised a hopper that could store dry earth, charcoal or ashes. A pull on the handle would release a sufficient amount of the hopper contents into the bucket. This was of great benefit to the ladies, and economical on the amount of soil being used. Ten years later the Reverend's invention was superseded by another. A man called Parker brought on to the market his Patent Woodstock Earth Closet. There was not even the need to pull a handle. When the user rose from the seat the removal of pressure activated some levers, releasing the exact amount of soil or ashes into the bucket.

Whether earth closet or bucket privy, it still had to be emptied. It was reckoned that if the hole in the ground was dug to the correct specification, a 'night soiler' would only have to be emptied once a year. But when that year did come to its end the family had a problem. The emptying was done with a very special long-handled scoop. It took a long time. Very often the householder would have to call in the help of a raker or gongfermor (from the Saxon 'gong', a privy, and 'fey', to cleanse) – or in Welsh, the pannwr or carthiwr.

It is a job that still exists. Today the raker or carthiwr serves people who are not on main drainage and have cesspits or septic tanks that need cleaning every few years. He travels around in a rather posh motor tanker equipped with a suction pump. He lowers a pipe into the cesspit and within

A special long-handled scoop was used to empty the privy.

minutes the job is done. In the 13th century a gang of 13 gongfermors took five nights to empty the cesspit of Newgate gaol in London. It was not a pleasant job but they were well paid, receiving £4 7s 8d!

There were great tales told of gongfermoring. Mr E. Williams of Llanefydd, near Denbigh, tells a good one. The local raker in his village when he was a youngster was giving a local widow's closet its annual MOT. To do this he would scoop the contents out through a hole in the back into a pyramid in the little yard. He would then scoop the smelly pyramid into a number of buckets he carried with him and take them off in his horse and cart.

On this particular day the widow lady heard all manner of swearing and cursing coming from the back quarters, so she went to investigate. Instead of shovelling the night soil into buckets for carrying away, the raker was working like a mad man and scattering it all over the yard.

'What do you think you're doing, James Jones?' asked the widow.

'It's my coat,' said James Jones, 'I put it on the wall before I went down into the pit and then the wind must have blown it on to the yard, and now it's somewhere underneath all this damn smelly stuff.'

'Stop your swearing at once,' said the now irate lady, 'and put all that stuff in the buckets. If it's your coat you are worrying about, I will fetch you one of my dear husband's old coats … a much nicer one than the one buried in there, I am sure.'

It's not the bloody coat I am worried about, missus,' the raker replied. 'It's me sandwiches in the pocket of it that I'm after.'

Bucket privies would have to be emptied once a week. Several people have written to tell me theirs were emptied early on Sunday mornings. I find it difficult to believe this kind of thing was done on the sabbath in Nonconformist Wales, or that such a task should be carried out by any man wearing his Sunday-go-to-meeting, one and only suit! But the act was certainly carried out when the fewest number of people were around. It was such a dirty, mucky, smelly thing for a man to have to do that I suppose the only relief was to joke about it.

Where there were large families Father would have to dispose of the contents of two buckets. One old friend wrote to tell me of the mucking out arrangements in his old home. He was one of four boys. It was always the middle two that did bucket duties. The eldest son was regarded somewhat as a deputy father, as he earned his own bread and part of theirs. My friend, the youngest, was seen as too small for the job – but only, as he was soon to find out, during the time when he wore short trousers. On that wonderful day when he was given his first pair of long trousers to go to the County school, he was told by his two middle brothers that now he was out of short trousers he would be able to take his turn on the weekly bucket emptying. The rule about the short trousers had something to do with the splashing from over-full buckets ...!

J. P. J. from Holywell recalls that when he was a child a good number of the council estate houses where he lived were serviced by a terrace of six toilets. The local council made itself responsible for the emptying and would ask for tenders from carters who possessed their own horse and cart. He recalled the time when the job was given to Will Dw Lal, a rather innocent old character who did odd jobs with his pony and cart.

A terrace of three.

When the young lads heard Will Dw Lal was the new Council Raker they decided to play a trick. They made a straw effigy of an old woman, dressed it in a grey cotton dress and a black straw hat with a carnation, and placed it on the seat of lavatory No 1. At nine o'clock on Friday evening they all hid behind the wall to await the arrival of the new raker. Will came and whoaed his pony to a stop, before bursting into the lavatory.

Loud giggles came from behind the wall when they heard Will apologising profusely.

'Sorry, madam, I didn't know anyone was in. You carry on, madam, and I will come back when I have emptied all the others.'

Twenty minutes later Will was back, only to find the old woman still sitting on the seat.

'Hold on, missus,' said Will. 'If you thought you were going to be as long as this, you should have taken a good dose of castor oil before coming here.'

[2]

COMING INDOORS

Men and women changed their ideas during the Renaissance. They changed their religion during the Reformation. They changed their work and their homes during the Industrial Revolution. But it seemed nothing could persuade them to change their lavatorial habits and construct a place of easement within their own homes. B. Rowlands of Anglesey tells me that as late as the 1960s Anglesey County Council had an official raker doing his weekly rounds in parts of Gaerwen. Mrs R.T. of Bwlchgwyn, writing about the same period, says:

'When you went to a dance on a Friday night, something that would happen about six times a year, you would have to walk past Frank and his stinking cargo and pretend you hadn't seen him.'

Inventors and science boffins had been working on the possibility of inside loos for years, centuries, before they began to appear in British homes. At the end of the 16th century Sir John Harington, Queen Elizabeth I's godson, had devised the first water closet, whereby water from an overhead cistern flushed the privy contents away. He even wrote the first Book of Privies, entitled *Metamorphosis of Ajax*. The Queen had one of the new inventions installed at Richmond Palace. But that was it. No one else paid a blind bit of notice.

Normally innovative ideas are taken up by the rich and influential, and as they become more common and cheaper they spread down to the hoi polloi. It could perhaps be argued that if His Lordship and Her Ladyship had been required to empty their own potties every morning, and My Lord Bishop required to do his own weekly night-soil raking, the indoor WC could have found earlier approval. But their lordships always had their paid servants to carry out those duties for them and they often relied on the chamber pot or close stool. In 1745 Dean Jonathan Swift wrote his *Direction to Servants,* in which he castigated the mistress who refuses to use the outside privy:

'I am so much offended with those ladies, who are so proud and lazy that they will not be at pains to step into the garden and pluck a rose [i.e. go to the garden privy], but keep an odious implement, sometimes in the bed chamber itself or at least in a dark closet adjoining, which they make use of to ease their worse necessities, and you are the usual carriers away of the pan, which makes not only the chamber but their clothes offensive to all who come near. Now to cure them of the odious practice, let me advise you, on whom this offis lieth to convey away this utensil, that you do it openly, down the great stairs, in the presence of footmen: and if anybody knocketh, to open the street door, while you still have the vessel in your hands: this if anything can, will make your lady take the pains of evacuating her person in the proper place [i.e. outside the house], rather than expose her filthiness to all the men servants in the house.'

As long ago as 1775 Alexander Cummings patented a usable water closet. And shortly after, Joseph Bramah designed a WC of the highest quality – no more nasty smells *and* efficient emptying. Thomas Crapper's late 19th-century inventions brought the controlled flush and the U-bend into the privy system. Then, during the 1800s WC bowls began to be produced by quality manufacturers like Doulton and Wedgwood and were to be found in the grandest of homes, and keeping up with the Joneses played its part in spreading the word.

An object of curiosity – an early WC bowl on display at Penrhyn Castle, Llandegai.

There was still a great deal of resistance to even the idea of having the privy come indoors. I was born in Blaenau Ffestiniog in 1918 and we certainly had mains water and mains sewerage for as long as I can remember. But the loo and its pull-chain equipment still remained in the yard outside.

Mrs Chloris Morgan of Bangor tells a tale from the mid 1960s. Two boys of a family had left home and their widowed father remained as the sole occupier. The house had just an outside tap and outside privy. When the lads had begun courting they had felt ashamed taking their girlfriends to witness such a primitive lifestyle. They decided to club together and pay for making the house completely 'mod con'. The old man was thrilled, right up to the time the contractors arrived and told him the Ty Bach was to be inside

A grand wooden closet, with an extra long chain, at Penrhyn Castle.

the house. There was confrontation and eventually confrontation turned to compromise. The new WC gear of cistern and porcelain pan was plumbed into the little place at the top of the garden and the house itself was left sweet and uncontaminated. 'Not hygienic to have a thing like that inside,' the old man had insisted.

I suppose one reason for the resistance of country people to change could have been their reluctance to waste the goodness that bucket contents and night soil carts brought to their gardens and to their fields. Why pay for artificial fertilisers when the real stuff was obtainable free in regular quantities from one's own privy?

People living in the western corner of North Wales always maintained that no potatoes in the world could be compared to Tatws Morfa Bychan in Merioneth, and Tatws Penmon in Anglesey. Yet I have it on good authority that delicious potatoes were nurtured in the olden days on good local night soil – genuinely organically grown.

There is another point too, that of privacy. My parish registers tell me that in those 'good old days' houses were small and families were large. A two-down and one-up cottage or terraced house would often be home to a large family – father and mother, perhaps six or seven children, and very often a granny in a black cotton frock and laced bonnet, sitting in the corner. Downstairs would be the living room and the siambar (chamber) or master bedroom. Father and mother and possibly one or two of the smaller children would occupy the master bedroom. The teenagers would sleep in the loft and Granny and the other children would sleep on straw in the living room behind that most cherished, most utilitarian and most versatile of room dividers, the Welsh dresser.

'A place apart' – Dave Morris at Ty Newydd, Penmachno. Many wanted to keep the privy outside and away from the house.

Yesterday's house lacked space. There was no place where one could be alone. The only bit of quiet a mother could enjoy were those few minutes in the day when she came to sit on the seat of the little place apart, that little island of peace in the garden. Even sitting on the seat of one of a row of urban loos that served a terrace of quarry or railway houses could in those days be bliss. And perhaps a chat with a neighbour through the thin partitioned wall, or during the walk to or from the little house, would be regarded as a treat that was not to be forsaken lightly.

No one will ever know what a great difference the lavatorial revolution will have had on the lives of people who no longer had to advertise publicly their comings and goings to that smelly, often rat-infested, little house at the bottom of the garden. Nor can we ever realise the difference its coming must have made to the well being of so many spinster ladies and people who were shy and withdrawn. Although so many of the older people who have written to me have described with warmth and affection the adventures and pranks of privy days, there must be thousands of others who found the whole idea of a bucket or potty full of poo, and muck rakers traversing their streets, repulsive.

And yet this is my opinion. Of all the letters I have received about the privies of the olden days, I had only one from a woman who 50 years on still shudders with disgust and abhorrence at the primitive way of life that her contemporaries were so reluctant to cast away. She wrote of her childhood and teenage years in Wrexham with much sincerity:

'My father was a blacksmith. We lived in one of three terraced houses built by my father. Our privy was in the backyard. I loathed this stinking earth closet which was emptied by a local man every Friday night and I hated using it on Thursdays when the contents threatened to touch my bottom. But when you have to go, you have to go.'

But even this honest lady could not resist just a little touch of nostalgia. She continued: 'The only time I felt happy in the loo was when I used it after my father. He was a big man with a big bottom. The seat was always warm after him and the place smelt of Coral Flake, a pipe tobacco he had smoked since he was 13 years of age and which cost elevenpence per ounce. I know the price because he used to send me to buy it for him and he always gave me the penny change.'

[3]

BUILDING AND MAINTAINING A PRIVY

R. P. Jones, of Llangernyw, is able to describe the making of a garden privy. He says that as the new house was being built all the surplus material would be set apart – the odd bits and endings of wood, roofing slates with a chip, and bricks that were a bit uneven. The site of the privy in the garden would have been chosen just as carefully as had been the site of the house itself. The direction of the prevailing wind would also have been noted.

The surplus materials would be carried to the site-designate of the Tŷ Bach, and when the house had been completed, the brickie/joiner would start work on the privy – the foundations, the walls, and the roofing. Then would come the day when the brickie/joiner would come and knock on the kitchen door of the newly built house and ask to see the missus. With downcast eyes, he would ask the inevitable question:

'I would just like to know, ma'am, whether you wish one, two, or three holes in the lavatory seat?'

'Two, I think, Mr Cadwaladr,' would be the shy answer. And the work would continue.

I don't remember a privy being built, but I was familiar with privy maintenance. Our local council in Blaenau Ffestiniog, Merionethshire was labelled Urban District. From as long as I can remember, as I have related, we had piped water and we were connected to a main sewer, but our loo remained in the yard below and was always kept spotlessly clean. My father was the cleaner-in-chief and from a very early age I was allowed to help.

A newly lime-washed privy.

I loved cleaning the loo with my father on Saturday mornings, and spring or special cleanings were also carried out quarterly. The ceiling and walls were then lime-washed with several coats. Because we lived in a town, we also had our own Urban Gas Works and their huge gasometers. The making of gas brought with it two main by-products, coke and coal tar. People would go with wheelbarrows, trucks, and old prams to buy the coke to burn in stoves and under the Monday morning wash-boiler. On Closet Springclean mornings my father would give me tuppence and a tin can and dispatch me to the gas works to buy a quart of coal tar. When the lime wash was dry, he would paint a foot wide dado along the bottom of the walls and purposely allow his generous brushfuls of coal tar to run on to the quarry-tile floor. The black and white decor looked good to the eye, it killed off creepy crawlies and it made the Little House smell like a hospital.

Blaenau Ffestiniog's main industry was slate quarrying. The slabs, before being split into slates, had to be slowly sawn with massive diamond-tipped saws. Throughout the process water had to be poured on to the slate to prevent the saws overheating. The water and the slate dust flowed into a trough and became known as 'baw cafn' or 'trough sludge'. This slate sludge mixed with water was often used as distemper paint. So, for the residents of Blaenau Ffestiniog, there was always a choice of privy decor. One could sit and meditate in a small black and white Ty Bach, or in a slate blue Little House with a mushroom coloured seat. I, personally, preferred the black and white decor.

As to toilet paper, I only remember as a child newspaper cut into squares, tied with string in one corner and hung on a nail in a convenient place. I have heard it said that some newspapers were regarded as being of a softer texture and more adaptable than others. But I never met anyone who would have chosen the *Daily Mail* or *The Times* as his daily newspaper just because at the end of the day it made for the easier cleansing of their nether end!

It was quite amazing to discover how many different kinds of birds and insects tenanted privies, especially the soil and bucket kind. Flies were a problem. They lived in droves near their favourite food supply and they brought with them their

Any type of paper could be used in the loo – preferably soft and with something to read on it!

predators. Spiders of various sizes and colours and breeds claimed all the nooks and corners for the setting up of their fly-catching gear. Then on late summer evenings the bats would hover and dive and the women would be terrified that, in spite of their radar system, the bats might occasionally miss and become entwined in their hair.

Both the soil and the bucket privies also attracted rats. It was because of the rats that one always coughed or whistled and made a noise on the way to the loo at night. Best let the rats know you were coming! But apparently not just rats. Tramps, or gentlemen of the road, were also quite fond of coming for a sit down in other people's loos after they had gone to bed. It made a change for them from having to crouch down in the hedge.

Mrs Lloyd, of Abergele, writes to say that her mother used to warn her to beware of snakes along the path during the summer months. We now live in a near snakeless environment. I remember coming to live in Llandegai, in 1952, and in the summer groups of boys would come to the churchyard to catch snakes. They all had to be told how to know the difference between the grass snake and the viper, or adder, because both kinds lived in the churchyard at that time. The grass snake became an affectionate pet, but the adder could land a person in a hospital bed.

It appears too that during cold winter nights privies gave shelter to a good number of man's furred and feathered friends. Mrs Megan Jones, of Dolgellau, writes:

'I am married to a farmer's son, but he is not a farmer. Soon after we were married his parents invited us to spend Christmas with them on the farm. We had goose for Christmas dinner cooked slowly on the Aga and I'm afraid I overdid things a little. In the middle of the night I had the

41

most awful collywobbles and had to take the dreaded path to
the garden privy behind the pig sties. I lit a candle, but ten
yards further the wind had blown it out and I was in too
much of a hurry to relight it.

'Eventually I got there, and sat down heavily on the seat. I
put my hands down to be more comfortable and they landed
on two roosting hens, one each side of me. I am certain my
scream would have been heard in the next village. It soon
brought my husband at the gallop to see what was wrong.'

Owen Jones, of Llangefni, has a stranger tale to tell. They
had a human privy nuisance. Mr Jones explains how every
well planned privy in the olden days would face away from
the house, with a gap of a foot or more for ventilation under
the door. The opening to theirs faced the low boundary wall
between their house and next door. Their next door
neighbour was a retired widower and his favourite hobby was
standing in his garden, with his elbows on the wall, his chin
cupped in his hands, and just staring at their privy door. If
any came to use the privy, he was always there with a greeting
and a little comment about the weather. They all felt that he
would be able to hear even the slightest noise they made
inside the privy. It was very unnerving. But the old man was
doing nothing wrong. It was his garden; it was his boundary
wall; and a cat can look at a queen. Owen Jones tells us how
things came to a head one dark evening in mid-October.

'My wife decided she wanted to go to the privy before
going to bed. I offered to accompany her but she said she
would be all right if I kept the back door open. But I did walk
up a little way and that was how I knew he was there. I heard
him saying to my wife, "Good evening, Missus! Nice evening.
Going to rain tomorrow, so they say." I couldn't hear what my
wife said to him. Then I heard the privy latch and the door
being shut. I moved a little nearer, seeing he was there.

'Then there was a most unearthly screech followed by a piercing scream from my wife. I ran up to the loo, and saw some wild creature scurrying like a tornado from under the door and jumping over our garden wall. I heard a dull thud and the old man next door fell to the ground and rolled down his own garden path.

'It was only after several cups of tea, laced with a bit of brandy, that my wife was able to tell me what had really happened. She had got into the privy and sat on the seat; she had then stretched her arm out and she touched some animal that obviously woke up and had spat at her before giving that piercing scream and escaping through the gap under the door.

'In the light of day we found that the animal in question was Simon, Mrs Williams No 5's Persian tortoiseshell. In his panic to get home he had jumped the wall and crashed head on into the old pensioner next door and had knocked him clean off his feet.'

Owen Jones ends by saying that the old man soon got over his experience. But strangely enough he never again came and put his elbows on the wall and cupped his chin in his hands and stared at their privy door.

The privy has always been the natural habitat for birds. They love to bag a place to build a nest in any kind of privy. Here there is shelter for the young and a constantly topped-up fridge of fresh luscious worms just by nipping down into the hole.

Mrs Gwen Hughes told me how a bird saved their privy from demolition: 'With the demise of the old plum tree last year the loo began to look like the proverbial sore thumb. But a wagtail made its nest just above the door. I planted ivies and creepers to soften the edges a little and now I am happy to say our lavatory looks wonderful in its new autumn coat.'

She goes on to say that some time later the newly landscaped loo was tenanted for several days by a wild goat. Mrs Hughes continues: 'Unfortunately the goat's aim was seriously bad and despite our loo being a two-holer he missed on every occasion – leaving the place in a terrible mess.'

[4]

PRIVY MYSTERIES

My first visit, as author designate, to an old fashioned loo proved just a little bit painful. The first to telephone me after my appeal in the *Daily Post* was my old farmer friend, Will Penbryn. He knew of a smallholding in Llanllechid, now unoccupied, that had a garden privy. He told me that both his brother and his sister Kitty had lived at this farm, Plas Ucha. When we arrived at the farm, however, we found it was derelict; the roof had caved in and the windows were boarded up. It had not been vandalised, but was just falling into decay. I thought how sad, and how brave of my old friend to have come with me to see what must have been for him such a woeful sight.

The privy of the ruined house was still standing intact and aloof. Its door was closed and its roof compact just as it must have been the day it was built. But it was guarded by a lush army of nettles, and I am allergic to nettles. Undeterred, my farmer friend Will picked up a fallen branch and cut a path through to the closet door much quicker than I would have done with a strimmer. And there it was – and it was occupied. A blackbird had built its nest on the one-holed seat.

That was the beginning. After this I was invited to enjoy viewing other one-holers, and two-holers, and three-holers, and even ten and twelve-holers, as I travelled the length and breadth of North Wales.

It was the three-holers that set the first problem. I had read that these had been built so that father and mother and child could all go along and perform together at the same time. I

Will Penbryn thrashing his way through the nettles to reach the privy at Plas Ucha.

The privy seat – occupied by a blackbird's nest.

A three-seater with holes designed for adults and a child.

couldn't accept this. It sounded so unnatural and so unwholesome. Anyway, what would the other eleven boys be doing whilst father Jacob and mother Rachel and father's blue-eyed boy, Joseph of the multicoloured coat, were all down in the loo together?

In fact the true explanation is far more complex. It is based on the assumption that the father's nether end is bigger than that of the mother, and that both are bigger than that of the child. It is also based on a little known geometrical theorem: 'The bigger the hole, the further the protrusion of a body sitting on it'. QED. If a small or a thinnish person sat on a large lavatory hole his bottom would be in danger of touching the contents of the bucket below. If, on the other hand, a large person sat on a small hole too distant from the bucket, there would be the danger of unpleasant splashes from below. I am sorry, but there have been so many misconceptions about three-holed loos that these things have got to be said!

The case for the two-holed privy is different. There are two different kinds of two-holers. Some have equal sized holes, others have different sized holes. The latter work on the same 'made to measure' idea as the three-holers, but are presumably for a smaller family. Those with two holes of the same size, however, work on an entirely different principle and would be found where there were large growing families.

The family would know that as from Sunday morning, or as soon as the buckets had had their weekly emptying, only the left-hand hole facing, was to be used. Midweek, father would make his weekly inspection and if he decided that No. 1 bucket was as full as it should be, he would set the cover on the left-hand hole facing and the family would know that, as from that moment, hole No.2 would be the one to use.

A two-seater with pear-shaped holes.

Father, at slop bucket emptying time, would have two buckets to carry, but this was preferable to having to make two separate journeys a week.

I soon found out that there was more to writing a book about privies than just doing the rounds, listening to funny little stories of yesteryear, and taking photographs. To do the job properly one had to have a fairly scientific mind. There were mysteries to be solved!

I was invited to several places that had two separate privies in their gardens. Some of the buildings were detached, others not. Some had a one-hole seat in each division; others had one hole in the first and two or three in the second.

By this time my project had had several mentions in newspapers and on radio. I had the feeling that people were beginning to regard me as a kind of garderobian authority.

The old chapel at Amlwch, Anglesey, and (*below*) the ruins of the privies, including the special one for the minister.

They somehow expected me to come up with the answers. Dual loos baffled me until I received a letter from a friend, Margaret Cooke, in Llandudno Junction.

She writes: 'My grandparents kept the Penrhyd chapel house in Amlwch. There were two well kept Ty Bachs in the garden. One was large and roomy and I thought it very posh. The other was smaller and plainer. I still remember the great difference between them to this day. The other day I visited my grandparents' grave and I also visited the old, by now ruined chapel. It, and the old shell of the house, and its loos still stand...'

But only just: because when I went there with my camera all the old buildings presented a very sorry sight.

In her letter, my correspondent proceeds to solve the Dual Loo Mystery: 'The posh loo,' she says, 'was for the visiting minister, whilst the other, the more humble one, was for the family.'

In Wales, most Nonconformist ministers are at home in their own chapels only on the first Sunday of the month. Visiting preachers, some from afar, take over the pulpits on the other Sundays. In pre-car days the visiting preacher would arrive on Saturday evening and return home on the Monday morning. Chapel members would normally vie with each other for the privilege of entertaining the visiting preacher. But it has to be said that some of the Reverend gentlemen tended to be a bit dry, straight laced, and plain boring, and for them the chapel secretary would have difficulty finding voluntary hosts.

These gentlemen would stay at the chapel house and become the guests of the chapel caretakers. They were provided with their meals and, strangely enough, church funds also provided a jar of tobacco for their use. It was called 'baco'r achos' or 'denominational tobacco'. Whether

The privies at Llangynhafal Old Rectory.

the minister chose to eat his meals with the family in the kitchen, or have them served to him in the privacy of the parlour would presumably be a matter for him. According to Miss Cooke, he had no such choice as to where he would ease himself after the meal. The large posh closet was for the minister's sole use – the smaller one would be for the family.

Mr and Mrs Arbuthnott, of Llangynhafal near Denbigh, then very kindly wrote to tell me they too had two privies in their garden, one with a single hole and next door a double. This was not a chapel house and yet it had the same mystery dual combination. But I was not put out because their letterheading read: 'The Old Rectory'. Chapel House! and Rectory! There could well be a connection, I thought. The next in line with a similar phenomenon to report was from that lovely old house called Pentir in the village of Carrog, near Corwen. This had a two-holer and back-to-back with it a

The two-holer.

corner seat one-holer. This house too was an old vicarage.

The Church in Wales never indulged in the chapel habit of changing of pulpits except perhaps for Harvest Festivals. So could the privies at the old vicarages have been built to accommodate the bishop when he came annually for the service of confirmation and/or the archdeacon when he came on his annual visitation? Then I heard of more and more of these dual privies in places not connected with Non-conformist ministers and clerks in holy orders. I have been forced to the conclusion that, as many of our present homes boast a guest bedroom so, in the olden days, many of our homes were proud to own a guest privy. Such luxury!

There could, of course, be another explanation. The little one-holers could have been for the maids. It just wasn't done to have the maid waiting her turn outside whilst the Reverend master of the house was meditating upon his next

53

The corner seat for servants.

The privy in Caerwys Rectory, Mold, is attached to the stables. It has a strong double seat and a deep window/lamp alcove to the side.

Sunday's sermon inside. Servants must have been a problem. Many people have written, some of whom had been in domestic service in their younger days, to tell me that: 'the maids were allowed to use the privy in the afternoons'. Disciplined bladders and bowels! What?!

[5]

INDUSTRIAL PRIVIES

Presumably from the beginning of time, Man would urinate and excrete just where and when he felt like it. There would be no question of attempting to cross legs until he came to the nearest public toilet. Nature provided millions of undertaker insects that would nibble and eat what his body rejected and return it into the earth through their own little bodies. But at some stage in his development, Man began to cultivate the emotions of shame and modesty and the feeling that it was not for him, a Homo Sapien, to be seen crouching and evacuating himself in public places. So Man decided that he would do his business in a place apart. It was then that all the problems of earth soiling and the emptying of buckets began.

Darwin, in his *Origin of Species*, tells us that evolution throughout the world was very uneven. Whilst development on one island almost exploded, it tended to remain static on another. Something similar must have happened in the slate quarries of North Wales!

Pre war, over 2,000 men worked in the Oakley Quarry in Blaenau Ffestiniog. Approximately half would work in the mills splitting and trimming the slates, whilst the other half worked in the underground caverns that are now such popular tourist attractions. The Oakley boasted of the deepest slate mine in the world, layer upon layer of caverns wending their way deeper and deeper into the ground in a network of tram lines.

In that vast, dark theatre underground where 1,000 men

The opening leading down into the Oakley Quarry mine.

worked by candlelight, from seven in the morning till half-past four, there was not a single lavatory, or latrine, where a man could stop and do his business. It was pitch dark in those caverns and when the call of nature came men stopped wherever they were, pulled their trousers down and did it just there – anywhere except on, or between, the tramlines.

It was nature that provided the quarry mine with its own scavengers. Every quarry mine had its thousands of rats, and no miner would kill a rat. The men used to walk in couples into the mines; they would link arms and walk the tramlines. Often they would see two small beady eyes coming towards them. The rats also walked the tramlines and would only give way to their food providers when they were within inches of each other.

I remember a story being told at the time of the appointment of a new under-manager. He was an engineer and had no prior experience of slate mines. He was also a golfer. One day in a lonely part of the mine he took a swipe at a rat coming to meet him. The rat gave out a piercing alarm scream and dozens of other rats rushed to its assistance. The new under-manager had a very lucky escape that day.

In contrast, the slate makers working above ground fared better. They had their own four- or five- or even six-holers within easy reach of the sheds in which they worked.

The ten-seater at Port Penrhyn, Bangor.

In Port Penrhyn, Bangor, there still remains the most beautiful privy that anyone could ever hope to see. Now a listed building, it's round and it's a ten-seater. There are ten ventilating round windows in the wall, one above each seating place, and the diameter of the windows and the diameter of the seat holes below are equal. Inside there is the most ornate wrought iron work. This in turn supports four massive polished slates that divide it into four segments. The segment by the door provides the vestibule area and a hole for one; the other three segments have three seats each. Old Ifan Pugh, who used to work as a slate packer in the Port, said to me: 'You should have heard the debates we used to have in there, Reverend! Some of those debates were far more interesting than the ones they have in the House of Commons in London.'

[6]

SCHOOL PRIVIES

I became the vicar of Llandegai in 1952. The village had two school buildings: the junior school on the left of the church, and the primary on the right. The junior school building had, and still has today, a small terrace of privies built over a stream. The little stream, and its contents, have run for many years into a huge mound of earth in the park below and disappears there. There is no smell, no unpleasantness, and no one can remember a time when anything went wrong with the junior school closets.

One ex-pupil, now 80 years of age, told me how, during the dinner break, he and his friends would go the closets and light paper boats. They would throw them down the pan and then rush out to the area where the stream was exposed and watch the little fire boats disappear into the underground tunnel.

Even in the mid 1950s the primary school, on the other hand, had to make do with four bucket lavatories housed in wooden sheds at the far end of the playing field. There were constant complaints from mothers. Perhaps Jenny had wet her knickers on the way home from school because she would not use the school lavatories, where the boys used to come and spy on them through the cracks in the planks. Parents also complained that some of the younger children were suffering from inflammation of the bladder, and attributed this to the cold winds that penetrated the privy sheds. Surprisingly, as chairman of the governors for well over 30 years, I don't think I heard a single complaint about the fact that they were *bucket* lavatories.

An old privy bucket – most schools had either these or earth closets.

Things finally came to a head and the local authority was forced to take action. Mrs Arthur Williams wrote a letter to the headmaster to say that she was keeping her Beryl home from school because she had an awful rash on her bottom. She went on to explain that her Beryl had gone to the school closet during play and that William Richard, knowing she was there, had stuck a nettle through the crack in the planks and it had caused a rash down her buttock and thigh.

It appears that this nettle business went on quite a lot in the privies of old. I also had a letter from Ivor Davies of Brymbo, Wrexham, reporting similar stings in the tail:

'Glyn Jones and I were apprentice joiners employed by local builder Ronnie Vaughan of Caergwrle in 1947. We were both 16 years of age. We were sent to work with Alf Parry and we had the task of making some windows. Our workshop was a disused stable situated within a property called White

House. Mr Parry, the owner of these premises, came to us a couple of days after we started work and said that he had only just realised that we had not got a toilet. He suggested that if we brushed out the long-disused earth closet at the bottom of the much overgrown garden, we could use it.

'Glyn was the first of us to use the toilet and when sitting comfortably, I selected a long nettle and reached in through the rear apperture of the building and touched Glyn's bottom with it. Glyn let out a yell and shouting that a rat had nipped him, raced down the garden with his trousers round his knees. Alf Parry, having seen what had taken place, lay doubled up on the ground with laughter.'

But to return to the saga of Llandegai. As a result of the nettle affair the buckets were removed and the pull-chain system was introduced in new lavatories inside the school. Boys on the left. Girls on the right. The term following the introduction of the Mod Cons, however, nearly 40% of the pupils suffered the most awful bout of sickness and diarrhoea. Many parents were also affected.

It became a pattern. At the beginning of every term came the dreaded sickness and diarrhoea. Some of the parents of new entrants, who caught the bug from their children and lacked the immunity we older parents had earned, were sick near unto death. It never came to the point where parents stood outside the school gates waving banners declaring 'Bring back the buckets' or 'New toilets out', but that was what was being said.

I arranged to meet the Medical Officer of Health in Caernarfon. Swabs were taken from all the children and from members of their families. The bug carriers, who never showed symptoms themselves, were identified and prevented from attending school until pronounced clear, and this was only after a period of absence of many months.

When the mystery was eventually resolved, the cause was found to be indirectly connected with the installation of the modern WCs. It appears that this had encouraged school staff to inaugurate a small hygiene campaign. Children were encouraged to wash their hands before the mid day school meal. They were also asked to bring their own face cloths and towels for this purpose. It was soon apparent that the infants class were too little to cope with this new function. They brought their face cloths and their towels, but most of them had no idea how to use them. The greatly harassed classroom assistant found that wiping and drying 30 small faces and 60 tiny hands, using 30 different face cloths and towels, within a stipulated period of time could not be done. So she settled for getting her tiny clients to queue in a line and giving each one a quick lick and a promise with the same communal face cloth and towel. After all those years with only the most basic of amenities, hygiene can sometimes be over done!

[7]

THE SMOKING PRIVY

It's Mrs Muriel Parry, from the Lleyn, who told me this story. Muriel and I have known each other for many, many years. When she heard I was writing a book about privies, she thought it only right I should have a good privy mystery to include in it.

Muriel told me that at the beginning of the First World War her uncle Tom, her mother's brother, had married a most peculiar woman. She was reputed to have come from South Wales. She certainly spoke as they do in the South, but apart from that no one knew a thing about her or how Uncle Tom had come to lay eyes on her. Tom was the first volunteer from the village to answer Kitchener's call. Many said, 'with good reason'. He came home five years later a sick and a broken man. When he died as a result of his war wounds six years later, he and Matilda had four children.

Matilda was sadistic in the way she treated her children; she threatened them, she beat them, and she meted out the most horrible of punishments for the littlest misde-meanours. And she was especially hard on Maldwyn. Maldwyn was the youngest and he was a little slow. He was terrified of his mother and had developed such a stutter that no one, except his grandfather, could understand a word he said. Maldwyn loved his grandfather, who lived near them, and when he was with him could converse without the slightest impediment.

The children grew up and left home to go as domestics or farm labourers at the earliest opportunity. Matilda bought the little village shop and used Maldwyn to haul the groceries on and off the shelves, and to dig the garden so that they had garden produce to sell. Things went on comparatively well. Maldwyn was now a young man. The constant nagging went on, but the frequent beatings had stopped.

It was around Maldwyn's 30th birthday that it happened. Matilda had been acting strangely, arranging and re-arranging the shelves long after closing time. One day a customer came in and complained that he had bought a packet of ten Woodbines the previous day and when he had taken it home and opened it, it had one cigarette missing. The next day there were several similar complaints, and there were pipe smokers complaining that their packets of shag had been tampered with. Matilda immediately blamed Maldwyn. She even took a stick and beat her poor terrified son as he pleaded his innocence with her.

That night Maldwyn crossed the road and visited his grandfather. 'Honest, Grandpa,' he said. 'I have never smoked in my life. It's her that's pinching the cigarettes and the 'bacco. I know she smokes cigarettes and she's also got a clay pipe.'

'How do you know?' asked Grandpa.

'Well, I've seen the clay pipe in her apron pocket,' said Maldwyn. 'And when she goes to the privy after tea, you can see the smoke coming out from under the door and through the little window.'

'Does she go to the privy the same time every day, Maldwyn?' inquired Grandpa.

'Yes, she goes five o'clock every night regular.'

'Right,' said Grandpa, 'this is what we must do to catch her red-handed, and you, Maldwyn, will have to do most of this yourself. Fill a bucket with cold water and hide it behind the privy. When you see your mother heading for the privy go round the back to where the bucket is. As soon as you see the smoke, but not before mind, grab your bucket, kick the privy door open, and throw the water over whoever is sitting on the seat. Do you understand me, Maldwyn?' Grandpa inquired. 'Throw the water over whoever is sitting on the seat.'

'But Grandpa, she'll kill me,' whined Maldwyn.

'No, lad,' said the co-conspirator, 'I will be there. I will have taken my place behind that old apple tree. But you see, Maldwyn, she must be caught red-handed before anyone will believe you. I shall be your witness.'

'But ...' began terrified Maldwyn.

'But nothing!' said his grandfather. 'If she says anything you will just have to say, "I threw the water because I thought the privy was on fire."'

The plan worked. Matilda went to the loo at the usual time. Maldwyn took his place by the bucket of water. From where he stood he could just see the peak of his gramps's cap behind the apple tree. There was a wait of a few minutes then billows of smoke came from under the door and through the tiny little window. Maldwyn sprang into action, kicked the door open, and heaved the bucketful of water in the direction of the privy seat. Within seconds Grandpa, the witness, was there by his side. There was no sound from Matilda. She just sat there, soaking wet, with her thin white hair in wisps down her awe-struck face. The wet, limp cigarette was still in its place between her lips and the clay pipe and a box of baccy lay on the lavatory seat beside her.

Matilda apparently never recovered from her near-drowning experience. Muriel also tells me that Maldwyn, aged 85, retired recently as the rather prosperous owner/manager of the village store.

[8]

PEDIGREE PRIVIES

There are already some, but not many, public loos and garden loos that have become listed buildings. These are the pedigree privies of North Wales.

Buildings are not all listed for their beauty or elegance, but because they represent something of our past. Listed buildings are not therefore necessarily nicer looking than the non-listed – but some are. I came across a very tranquil and peaceful privy at Benar, in Penmachno, near Bettws y Coed.

This particular closet, built over a stream, is listed and its 'papers' give full details:

'Lavatory house, probably mid C19. Local flat rubble: thick slate roof. Centrally placed double wooden doors. Gable end to NW and SE; that to SE has small square window, that to NW has blocked square window. Building built into slope of ground which drops steeply down to stream at rear. Stream flows through square headed openings in the lower part of gable walls. Interior has two-seater latrine with wooden seats overhanging stream which carried away waste.'

The papers also give its grid reference, its graded reference, the date it was listed, and its record number. This information is all carefully filed in the offices of CADW.

Two other beauties I visited are right on the side of the main road on Marford Hill near Wrexham. It is easy to miss them if one is not looking for them. They are circular and probably date from the early 19th century. A lane now separates them from Beechmount, but they are said to be in the 'picturesque style' of the Marford Travalyn Estate when it

The peaceful privy at Benar, and its owner Dave Marshall.

The stream at Benar flowing into and through the privy.

The pair of round privies at Marford Hill, and the author's grandson Dafydd discovering what it was like to have to wait outside!

was under the stewardship of John Boydell. They are listed as of 'painted brick, pair of circular former privies with entrances with cambered heads and replaced conical roofs.'

There is a listed public lavatory at Blaenau Ffestiniog. This one had a pedigree chart longer than that of the Crufts Champion of Champions! The buildings were opened in 1866 as a terminus for the narrow gauge Porthmadoc to Blaenau Ffestiniog Railway. It was in use by the railway until 1932, but was then adapted as a public lavatory. It became listed 'for its special interest as a former railway station associated with the slate industry.'

Its pedigree papers describe in some detail its archi-

The listed public lavatories at Blaenau Ffestiniog.

tectural delights – 'Snecked rubble with dressed quoins and moulded string course over centre openings; yellow brick surrounds. Slate roof with fish scale patterning, clay ridge tiles and red/yellow patterned brick stacks. Ironwork cusping to bargeboards. Slate gable plaques with Prince of Wales Feathers carved by Robert Roberts, poet and carver, over cambered and droved lintels to recessed boarded doorways . . .' and so on.

When I turned up at Blaenau Ffestiniog to take a photograph of these seemingly palatial buildings, there were lots of people around. The car park had been cleared to make room for the once weekly open market. The older and more interesting part of the building was the section the women were using as their toilet. On this particular day there was a good deal of to-ing and fro-ing taking place at the Ladies entrance. I unpacked my camera, began to focus it,

71

The Prince of Wales Feathers at Blaenau Ffestiniog.

'Ironwork cusping' – the reality behind dry words.

and at this point I had the distinct feeling that a young WPC was eyeing me rather suspiciously. I promptly replaced my camera in its case and beat a quick retreat. I had visions of the *Daily Post* headlines the next day!

This did mean another 60 mile round trip accompanied by my daughter, as official photographer, the following day. Perhaps this was just as well, because with no immediate danger of being arrested I was able to concentrate on the building, including the Prince of Wales Feathers carved by Robert Roberts, poet and carver. And perhaps I would never have discovered what architectural beauty is hidden in the words, 'Ironwork cusping to bargeboards'!

[9]

NEAR-ROYAL PRIVIES

North Wales has its pedigree privies and it also has its near-royal privies. There is one of these at Penygwryd Hotel, Capel Curig, at the knee of majestic Snowdon. It was originally a farm. When it became fashionable for the rich and the famous to take up mountain walking, and later climbing, Farmer Owen turned his farm into a rather rough kind of self-catering hostelry. He would meet his guests at Bettws y Coed railway station and trundle them all the way in his horse and cart to his Penygwryd eagle-nest home.

In 1946 life changed for the farmer/innkeeper when he

Their Majesties King George VI and Queen Elizabeth meeting the architect Clough Williams-Ellis at the Penygwryd Hotel in 1946.

was told that King George VI and Queen Elizabeth were to visit Penygwryd to scrutinise the plans for the siting of the first National Park. They were to stay for one hour; but what, thought entrepreneur Owen, if His Majesty, or worse, his young queen, should ask to be taken to the toilet, and he Owen be required to escort them to the hotel's only place of convenience – the outside privies?

Immediately, the finest of porcelain seats, and all other lavatorial appurtenances, were ordered from Bangor, together with a plumber to erect them – this time inside the house itself. History does not relate whether or not this hastily erected closet can rightfully be designated royal, but it undoubtedly qualifies as a near-royal.

From the 1950s, under the management of Mr and Mrs Chris and Jo Briggs, Penygwryd became an internationally known hostelry for climbers, the Savoy of Snowdonia. It was

The demoted privy at Penygwryd Hotel, Capel Curig.

here that Hillary, Hunt and Evans and Sherpa Tenzing came to practise and to plan their conquest of Everest. It would certainly be true to say that most of those whose names appear in the Who's Who of famous climbers will have used the Penygwryd loo in their day.

The Cernioge of today is a beautiful farmhouse on the A5 road between Pentrefoelas and Cerrig y Drudion. It was once the Crewe Junction of coaching days, one of the main stage-coach stopping places between London and Holyhead.

Stage-coach routes had their many stops. Horses were changed every seven miles, but the farriers who changed the horses were as adept at their work as the grand prix pit mechanics of today. The change was made within minutes and very often travellers wouldn't even bother to come out of the coach and stretch their legs at these halts.

Cernioge was different. Horses and coaches were given a sort of routine MOT at Cernioge. A staff of farriers would stand at the ready to examine the horses; blacksmiths and wheelwrights would carry out coach repairs. All travellers would disembark and enter the magnificent house that was then almost three times as large as it is today. They would be refreshed and sustained by its ample supplies of ale and roast beef. Young Queen Victoria, when she came to Cernioge on her journey from Wynnstay to Beaumaris, drank tea in one of its sitting rooms and there is a plaque on the wall to record the fact.

There is no chronicled evidence that the Queen did use the lovely four-holed privy in the grounds of Cernioge. But she did drink tea at Cernioge; and she would still have had a further 30 miles and more to travel before arriving at her destination, Beaumaris! It is anyway fair to assume that Cernioge qualifies as a near-royal. The place even today has that kind of look about it.

Every stage-coach driver relied on milestones such as this between
stopping places.

Few people realise that Cernioge today is simply a farmhouse on the A5 road. It displays a plaque inside recording the visit of Queen Victoria.

If one is to define a royal privy as a place where a monarch took easement, then the privy at The White Lion Royal Hotel in Bala qualifies. There is strong evidence that Queen Victoria, many years after her stay at Cernioge, did actually use this particular toilet. Queen Elizabeth I is famed for the number of different beds she is alleged to have slept in. Poor Queen Victoria seems to break the monarchical record for the number of different places she is alleged to have used to perform other bodily functions.

Mrs Prescott, the proprietor of The White Lion Royal Hotel, tells the tale of how the Queen felt a sudden call of nature while walking along the main street of Bala.

The ladies-in-waiting had a hurried emergency meeting and the Queen was hustled to the nearest decent public building within sight. She was marched through the hotel corridors and up the stairs to the elegant new toilet that was

The near-royal privy at Cernioge.

79

Another near-royal – The White Lion Royal Hotel in Bala.

the hotel's pride and joy. The chief lady-in-waiting closed the door and Her Majesty was left to do as Her Majesty pleased.

Other hostelries offering the same service to monarchs along the centuries have been dubbed 'Royal': The Royal Oak Hotel, The Royal Sportsman, The Royal Ship. The White Lion in Bala was not allowed this distinction. It appears that a place could be deemed royal only if it gave or sold goods or services to the monarch by appointment. The necessity in Bala that day was so great there was no time for the formality of an appointment. So the hotel that should have been The Royal White Lion Hotel had to be content with being called The White Lion Royal Hotel instead.

[10]

RESCUE AND RENOVATE!

As soon as it became known I was writing a book about privies, I had invitations to see some that were in the process of being renovated by proud owners.

I visited the Hughes family in Ockbrook, Amlwch Port, Anglesey. They had modernised their house and had also very sensitively renovated their garden privy. For years, after it had ceased to be a privy, their now grown-up daughters had used it as super Wendy house. There had also been odd times when it had served as a 'shop' and as a 'hospital' and on

Angharad Hughes of Ockbrook, Amlwch Port, standing outside the two-holer in their garden, for years her 'Wendy house'.

occasion, when one of the smaller girls had had a crush on the vicar, as a 'church'. Angharad, when she was eight years old, had taken ages handsewing a curtain for its one window.

Quite naturally, therefore, after completing the modernising of the house, efforts had to be made to rescue the other little building that had served the family so well over several generations. Mr Hughes was able to carry out the work himself, but the difficulty was re-roofing. All the North Wales privies were originally roofed in North Wales slates and they, even in North Wales, are very expensive to buy.

Leri Roberts from Porthmadoc wrote to say that her redundant Ty Bach used to double as a hospital and as a zoo. The only creature that lived in her zoo, apparently, was a huge spider that she had grown very fond of. She would hurry home from school and make straight for the old privy and catch flies to place in her spider's web. She had come to believe that her spider knew her because he would always await her, sitting smugly in the centre of his web, at the same time every day, and he almost ate her dead fly offering from out of her hand. She also remembers being obsessed by the idea that her spider would die if she was not around to feed him.

My next port of call where I was made welcome, was Tal y Cefn Isaf, in Llanfihangel Glyn Myfyr, Cerrig y Drudion. Gerald Barber, the owner occupier, is a retired surveyor and was lovingly resuscitating his old three-seater privy. Mr Barber also complained about the cost of slates; but of course it would be sheer vandalism to have to crown a reborn loo with corrugated iron!

Mr and Mrs John Arbuthnott were renovating two privies in

The privy at Tal y Cefn Isaf, coming to life again.

Inside the old three-seater.

'Before' at Pentir, Carrog . . .

. . . and 'after', the old privy has become a smart outdoor eating area.

their garden at the Old Rectory, Llangynhafal. During my privy project, I have come across so many lovely old vicarages and rectories. This one with its delightful grounds was a gem. Soon the newly renovated privies will become the focal point of their home and garden. We clergy have never been too well paid, but by golly we have made up for it by having such lovely homes to live in!

But the restoration gem was the one at 'Pentir' (another old vicarage) at Carrog village on the banks of the river Dee, near Corwen. It was a boiling hot day when I called and the only member of the family at home was Hywel Lebbon, who was in the midst of his A-Level exams. Without even asking, he popped into the house and made the best pot full of tea I have ever had. Hywel then took me to see his father's 'rebirth of an old privy'. It was magnificent.

The main closet was a two-holer with an almost new looking seat with pear-shaped, equi-sized holes. Excavations in the back brought to light another one-seater privy back-to-back with the first and served by the same night soil hole. Hywel's father, with a stroke of genius, had incorporated the old closets into a delightful outdoor eating shelter.

It's not just the price of slates that puts people off rescuing their Ty Bach. It's this lurking fear that some fool will come after them and bulldoze the whole thing away again. This is a problem. But it is a problem that has a solution.

It has come as quite a shock to many people to discover how very few of the old privies remain in North Wales. Charles Pugh, Assistant Historic Buildings Representative of the National Trust, writes:

'I have been searching for information which might help you with your book, and have quickly discovered that due to their very nature, privies are inevitably the first victims of every ripple of modernisation. For example, I have been very surprised to discover that out of more than 100 habitations on the Ysbyty Estate, only six privies survive to this day.'

The privies of North Wales are becoming fewer year by year. They are our little museums of the past. They are part of our heritage, and our social history. So let it be known that those which remain can be preserved if they are registered as Listed Buildings. CADW sent me a roll call of ten listed privies in South Wales and five in North Wales; perhaps the publication of this book will set alarm bells ringing.

Authority lays down that it would consider for listing buildings that are of 'historic interest: this includes buildings which illustrate important aspects of the nation's social, economic, cultural or military history.' Our garden privies have been doing this for generations.

Gilfach Goch, Llanbedr near Barmouth, with its protective wall – the privy builders of yesteryear certainly meant their creation to last!

Or they should be buildings 'with a close historical association with people or an event of importance to the Welsh Nation.' What buildings could be of more importance than those like the one at Port Penrhyn, where better debates were heard, so they say, then even those in the House of Commons in London? And indeed, of more importance than all the little garden privies where countless fathers had a quiet smoke under the apple tree at night whilst guarding their womenfolk for the last rite before going to bed?

Toilets normally qualify for a Grade II listing as 'buildings of special interest which warrants every effort being made to preserve them.' Anyone can apply to have their toilet surveyed and listed, and if this is allowed and his mongrel possession is declared a pedigree, the owner will be presented with its papers. And the reward?

'Before a listed building can be altered, extended or demolished, listed building consent must be obtained from the appropriate planning authority. It is a criminal offence to alter, extend or demolish a listed building without listed building consent.'

There is also a clause in the act which says that: 'A listed building may qualify for a grant to aid repair work but this is not automatic.' Privy owners would be well advised not to hold their breath over this one.

And the answer to the final question is 'No'. If your privy is ever made a Grade II Listed Building you will not be required to have busloads of school children, on educational tours, trampling through your flower beds. It will still be your very own little private place to share with chosen friends.

So if you are the proud owner of a Ty Bach, please do cherish it and treat it with tender loving care. There are many of us here in North Wales who have the utmost affection for this small part of our social history.

A Privy by Any Other Name

It does amaze me that some of my fellow writers on privies – English ones – are able to list more than a hundred names that are used to describe the common privy. We in North Wales are far more conservative and more limited in our terminology. And if I may say so, we are also a little more delicate in our way of describing things pertaining to the posterior parts of our bodies than our friends across Offa's Dyke. We refuse to use what we regard as rather crude Anglo-Saxon terminology. I can think of only a few privy names that are in common usage:

Buckingham Palace
Closet
Nymbar 10 – 'Number 10' (presumably Downing Street)
Tŷ Bach – 'The Little House' (by far the most popular)
Tŷ Cyffredin – 'The House of Commons'
Y Cefn – 'The Back Quarters'
Y LLe Chwech – 'The Sixpenny Place' (the second most popular name, I would think. During my first week of researching this book I was invited to talk on Radio Wales. Hywel Gwynfryn was the interviewer and his very first question to me was: 'Tell me, Aelwyn, why do Welsh people call the privy 'Y LLe Chwech', The Sixpenny Place?' I was absolutely stumped and I have never found out)
Y Peti (this is possibly peculiar to Anglesey and could, according to Robin Parry of Rhos Meirch, have been used to describe dual loos)

ACKNOWLEDGEMENTS

I have always associated writing a book with sitting uncomfortably on an upright chair, staring bleary eyed at the screen of a word processor and being surrounded by a bevy of reference books and odd bits of information on assorted bits of paper. Writing a book about privies has been different. It has meant being out with my camera in the fresh air and it has also meant meeting people and making new friends. The writing of this book has given me real pleasure, and I have learnt such a lot in the process. For this I would like to thank:

That great host of kind people who are fortunate enough to still own a privy in their garden. They were kind, and they were hospitable.

My gratitude, too, to the many who having seen my appeals for information in their local papers, and heard them on their radio, so promptly put pen to paper and sent me their memories and their lovely little tales about the privies of their younger days. I hope I haven't spoiled any of them in the telling.

Then there is my old friend Chloris Morgan, herself an author, writer, and reviewer of many books. She always reads the proofs of everything I write. She has long come to the conclusion that I must have been away with chickenpox or whooping cough on those days when spelling, syntax and punctuation were being taught at my school.

Thanks are also due to those august institutions we have in Wales that have all been so helpful:

CADW-Welsh Historic Monuments

National Museums and Galleries of Wales

The National Library of Wales

The National War Museum

Gwynedd Archaeological Trust

The National Trust

The Royal Commission on the Historical Monuments of Wales.